IMAGES
of America

PONCA CITY
AND KAY COUNTY
BOOM TOWNS

The 17-foot tall bronze Pioneer Woman Statue stands between Marland's Grand Home on Grand Avenue in Ponca City, and the Marland Mansion to the northeast. E.W. Marland, who financed the sculpture, solicited models from 12 different artists. The models were displayed around the country and 750,000 people voted for their choice of the best representation of the pioneer woman spirit. This statue, the winner, depicts a pioneer woman in a simple, ankle-length, long-sleeved dress, wearing a bonnet and well-worn boots as she strides purposely toward the future. She is leading her young son by her left hand and carrying a Bible in her right hand. The statue was dedicated on April 22, 1929, with Oklahoma humorist Will Rogers as the main speaker.

IMAGES
of America

PONCA CITY
AND KAY COUNTY
BOOM TOWNS

Clyda R. Franks

ARCADIA
PUBLISHING

Published by Arcadia Publishing
Charleston, South Carolina

Library of Congress Catalog Card Number: 2002103981

For all general information contact Arcadia Publishing at:
Telephone 843-853-2070
Fax 843-853-0044
E-mail sales@arcadiapublishing.com
For customer service and orders:
Toll-Free 1-888-313-2665

Visit us on the Internet at www.arcadiapublishing.com

A few pump jacks, some separators, and storage tanks are all that remain of the hundreds of oil wells that once dotted the Three Sands Field. Eventually producing oil or natural gas from 14 separate horizons, Three Sands became one of the greatest producers of casing-head gasoline in America. In an effort to protect the natural gas horizons from waste, Three Sands became the first field in Oklahoma to adopt the general use of rotary rigs, introduced in the field by the Southwestern Petroleum Company, which allowed the gas production to be mudded off. Note the denuded area in the foreground resulting from uncontrolled salt water and oil releases. (Author's personal collection.)

CONTENTS

ACKNOWLEDGMENTS

Many of my childhood memories are of Ponca City; visiting the Pioneer Woman Statue, swimming at Wentz pool, taking dance lessons from Jackie Troup, and attending school in nearby McCord Elementary School.

It was with pleasure that I accepted the opportunity to return to this area to do research for this book. However, books are not written by any single person. They are a cumulative effort by many people, and this is no exception. Kay County is fortunate to have some incredible historians ensconced in its museums, cultural centers, and libraries.

Marilee Helton and Eleanor Hays at the McCarter Museum of Tonkawa History provided a wealth of information and photographs. Ann Ganer, Viola Tremble and Louise Parker at the Top of Oklahoma Historical Society's Museum in Blackwell shared their knowledge of the Blackwell oil field and many of the photographs in this book.

We raided the archives at Marland's Grand Home/Ponca City Cultural Center with the help of Darlene Platt. Karen Ley at the Oklahoma Historical Society's Pioneer Woman Museum helped sort through hundreds of pictures. Karen Dye, director of Newkirk's Main Street Association, provided valuable assistance and information.

Sharon Jordan and Alice Holmes put up with our numerous visits to the Marland Mansion and Kathy Adams, executive director at the mansion, provided us with reams of information and photographs. All of these women deserve a huge thank-you for their willingness to share the pieces of history entrusted to their care.

Special thanks go to Paul Waffle and Conoco Inc., Kathy Tribble at Phillips Petroleum Company, the Oklahoma Heritage Association, and to Fred Marvel, the terrific photographer with the Oklahoma Department of Tourism and Recreation, who has always come through for me.

Finally, thanks to my historical consultant, mentor and friend—my husband, Dr. Kenny A. Franks.

INTRODUCTION

The search for hidden wealth is an enduring theme of historical literature. Man is always searching for quick riches. Near the turn of the twentieth century, the search for black gold was launched. The most productive of the great oil booms began in the Indian Territory, which in 1907 joined with Oklahoma Territory to become the state of Oklahoma.

During the first 35 years of the twentieth century, Oklahoma produced 3,906,012,375 barrels of crude valued at $5,280,007,477—more wealth than all minerals extracted from California or Colorado. Much of that wealth was found in the north-central part of Oklahoma, Kay County.

This quest for black gold gave rise to one of the most dramatic periods in Oklahoma history, the era of the oil boom town. There were three types of boom towns. Some, such as Whizbang, were a direct result of a new oil find and owed their existence to oil. Others had been quiet farming communities before being swept up in the rush for oil. Overrun by thousands of people hurrying to the latest strike, they quickly lost their rural character and became roaring boom towns. Others still, such as Ponca City, already were established commercial centers prior to the discovery of nearby oil.

The tremendous drilling activity required a large number of workers. Thousands of skilled and semiskilled men, along with common laborers, were needed to fuel the boom. Many of these newcomers were young, unmarried men attracted by the prospect of high wages, and they wasted little time in spending their money. This in turn brought a hoard of honest merchants, gamblers, workers, hijackers, millionaires and prostitutes who competed side by side for their share of the riches.

When the cycle of creation, boom and decline ended, the fate of the boom towns differed. Some simply disappeared. Others were assimilated by nearby towns. A few, such as Ponca City, continued to grow once the boom ended, transforming themselves into national and regional energy centers.

Nothing but a collection of clapboard, shotgun houses and false-fronted businesses, the town of Three Sands straddled the Kay-Noble county line. The most prominent building in this photograph, taken from the top of the Sawyer No. 14 well, is the combination grocery store and meat market in the center of the picture. In the left foreground, a local resident can be seen walking back to his shotgun house from an outhouse. (Courtesy Western History Collection, University of Oklahoma Library.)

One

THE FIELDS

The oil development of Kay County, Oklahoma, was a dramatic leap westward from the already proven areas in the Osage and around Cushing. Legendary oilman Ernest Whitworth Marland, who started his oil fortune in Pennsylvania, visited the area around Ponca City in 1908 and secured a lease on the Miller Brothers' 101 Ranch. Although few oilmen had seriously examined the area, Marland had some indication there was black gold beneath the land.

Although Marland's initial well, the first oil well drilled west of the Osage Reservation, was abandoned, his second well was completed as a gasser in the spring of 1910. His ninth well, the Willie Cries for War No. 1, opened the pool to oil production and the oil rush to Kay County was on.

Oilmen began penetrating the region as early as 1911, around Dilworth. That field was extensively drilled and as oilmen pushed the proven area southward, it eventually merged with the Blackwell Field to the south. Kay County entered the history books in 1913, when the discovery well of the Mervine Field was completed with an initial flow of one hundred barrels per day. In 1916, the Marland Oil Company opened the North Newkirk Field with a gas well that flowed 2,000,000 cubic feet of natural gas daily.

These finds paled before the huge discovery south of Tonkawa along the Kay-Noble county line in the spring of 1921, when the Three Sands Field opened to production. By 1923, the royalty interest at Three Sands was estimated at $100,000,000.

9

A crew drills for water on the 101 Ranch in Kay County. The man in the center is turning a crank to pump water into the tub. In 1894, Marcus McClaskey struck natural gas at 90 feet while drilling a water well on his farm along Possum Creek in what was to become the Newkirk-Mervine Oil Field. (Courtesy Marland's Grand Home.)

When Marland first arrived in Ponca City in 1908, he moved his family into the Arcade Hotel at First Street and Grand Avenue, where they lived until 1911. During this period, his financial resources were limited and he could afford to hire only those workers who were absolutely essential for drilling operations. He paid V.H. Waldo, his driller, $6.00 a day, from which Waldo had to pay his crew. (Courtesy Marland Mansion.)

The home of George Nix (left center) in the midst of the Blackwell oil field has a cedar-lined driveway leading to the section line road. Muddy ruts lead from Nix's house to the nearby oil wells. Oil-stained water in a creek flows across the road to the right of Nix's house. The problem caused by rain and mud made moving heavy equipment difficult in the Blackwell Field. (Courtesy Top of Oklahoma Museum.)

Located ten miles northwest of Newkirk, Dilworth was granted a post office on March 17, 1917. Development of the town started after the discovery of the Dilworth oil field in 1911, and by the middle of the decade it was a thriving community. The town was platted by W. Matthews and John A. Frates, of the Dilworth Townsite Company, who purchased the 60-acre townsite from Charles Dilworth, a local farmer. (Courtesy Top of Oklahoma Museum.)

11

The Dilworth oil field was opened in 1911, and quickly attracted the attention of such oilmen as Lew Wentz, Harry Sinclair, and E.W. Marland. Marland was the most active oilman in the development of the field, completing 37 wells, 21 of which were gassers. Many of the wells were shallow and were drilled by cable tool rigs, utilizing wooden derricks such as those shown here stretching northward toward the Oklahoma-Kansas border four miles north of the town of Dilworth. (Courtesy of Top of Oklahoma Museum.)

The Myra No. 1 well in the Dilworth oil field was a typical cable tool drilling rig. The walking beam can be seen just above the roof in the center. The boiler in the shed turned a bull wheel that raised and lowered the walking beam. The end of the walking beam inside the rig raised and lowered the drill bit in the hole as it alternately rose and fell, allowing the bit to pound its way through the earth. (Courtesy Karen Dye.)

Cable tool rigs were used on many of the more shallow wells in Kay County. A steam boiler turned a bull wheel that operated a walking beam, which alternately raised and lowered the massive steel bit shown here being lowered into the hole, as it pounded its way through the earth. Periodically a bailer was lowered into the hole to clean out the cuttings. In this photograph the bailing has probably just been completed as one of the roughnecks is pushing the bit over the entrance in the hole in preparation for it being lowered. Because cable tool rigs were used on shallow holes the weight of the drilling equipment was not as heavy as that used on rotary rigs and the wooden derricks, as seen here, were sufficient to support the weight. (Courtesy Phillips Petroleum Company.)

This photograph was taken looking toward the north of the R.E. Welsh No. 14 well in the Dilworth Field. The field, which was discovered in 1911, was along the banks of Bitter Creek and its tributary, Spring Creek, in northern Kay County just south of the Oklahoma-Kansas border. Note the oil covered slush pit on the right with the remains of an old bull wheel on the bank. (Courtesy Top of Oklahoma Museum.)

A truck loaded with heavy pipe is making its way through the Dilworth Field past a row of shotgun houses. Note the myriad tracks leading off the main road to the wells. Such unimproved roadways became quagmires during the rainy season. The drilling rig in the center is covered with oil. To its left is an earthen oil storage pit. (Courtesy Top of Oklahoma Museum.)

14

This is a view looking north along the main street of Dilworth. Dilworth's population peaked at an estimated four thousand people during the oil boom era; yet by February of 1924, after the oil boom has passed, its inhabitants numbered only 71. The post office was closed on March 30, 1929. (Courtesy Top of Oklahoma Museum.)

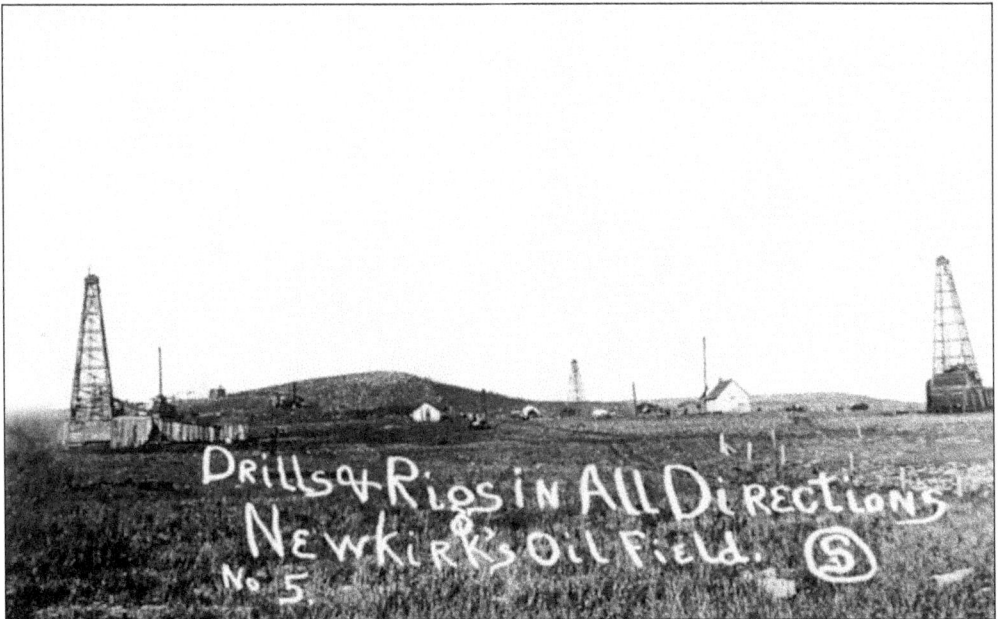

The first sign of oil and natural gas around Newkirk was made by M.E. McClaskey, who hit natural gas while digging a water well in the winter of 1893. McClaskey piped the gas into his house for use in heating and cooking. In 1898, the Newkirk Oil and Gas Company drilled a well on McClaskey's farm. It was the first commercial oil well in Oklahoma Territory. (Courtesy Newkirk Community Historical Society.)

The Bement wildcat well, pictured here, was in the Watchorn Field on the 101 Ranch lands along the boundary between southwestern Kay and northeastern Pawnee County. Opened in 1915, the Watchorn Field was named for Robert Watchorn, a major developer of oil and natural gas in Kay County. (Courtesy Marland Mansion.)

The discovery well of the Three Sands Field was one of the first successes of the geological method of investigation. However, Marland's discovery well, completed June 29, 1921, just barely missed being a dry hole. His second well produced 250,000 barrels of oil within four months. Living conditions were still primitive. Note the tent on the left and the tarpaper shack just to the right of the automobile. (Courtesy Marland's Grand Home.)

A forest of oil drilling rigs made up the Three Sands Oil Field. The production in the field was so prolific that the Marland and Cosden oil companies once paid $1,300,000 for a 400-acre lease. There was no well-spacing and so many wells were drilled that the legs often overlapped. Note how close the two rigs in the upper right are to one another. (Courtesy McCarter Museum of Tonkawa History.)

The discovery well at Three Sands was the Thomas No. 1. Horse-drawn wagons hauled drilling equipment south from Ponca City in the spring of 1920 for a ten-well drilling program. The first nine wells were dry holes. The tenth well, the Thomas No. 1 was completed as a 200-barrel per day well on June 30, 1921, and ushered in the huge production of the Three Sands Field. (Courtesy Pioneer Woman Museum.)

17

Workers, using teams and drags, are back-filling several newly constructed pipelines running to the wells in the Three Sands Field. The field became a maze of crisscrossing pipelines as production peaked in 1925 at 22,722,000 barrels of crude. By the close of the first half of the twentieth century Three Sands had produced 124,610,000 barrels of oil. To handle this outpouring of oil, 26 major pipelines, with a daily capacity of 185,000 barrels, and tanks capable of holding 1,000,000 barrels of oil were built. (Courtesy McCarter Museum of Tonkawa History.)

Workers on the Comar Oil Company School Land Lease are preparing to erect a wooden oil storage tank at Three Sands. The planks were placed upright and held together by steel bands. Oakum was then driven between the planks to seal them. However, most wooden tanks leaked. To plug leaks, workers would throw manure into the oil tanks. The manure would work its way to the leak and plug the hole. (Courtesy McCarter Museum of Tonkawa History.)

Sam McKee, whose farm was in the middle of the Three Sands Field, donated land to the United Brethren on which they built the Prairie View Church. Other denominations were free to use the church whenever it was not being used by the Brethren. Adjoining the church was the local cemetery, both pictured here. Within a short time, oil derricks had sprouted next to the fence surrounding the church and cemetery. (Courtesy McCarter Museum of Tonkawa History.)

Twenty-two wells are visible in this view of the original 160-acre lease owned by E.W. Marland in the Three Sands Field. In July of 1921, Marland organized the Comar Oil Company to operate his Three Sands holdings. In September of that year, Roxana Oil Company, a subsidiary of Royal Dutch-Shell, paid $2,000,000 for 51 percent of Comar's productive leases. The

money was used to acquire additional leases in Three Sands and by 1925, the Comar-Roxana partnership controlled 1,900 acres in Three Sands, which amounted to more than half of the field's total output. (Courtesy Pioneer Woman Museum.)

Fires were the curse of Three Sands. Fourteen oil storage tanks of the Comar Oil Company once caught fire and burned. Civil War-era cannon were used to fire solid shot through the sides of the tanks to allow the oil to drain off before it boiled over the top. (McCarter Museum of Tonkawa History.)

A combination of wooden drilling rigs (foreground) and steel derricks (background) could be found in the Three Sands Field. The wooden derricks were used to tap into the pool's more shallow fields. The stronger steel skeletons were necessary to support the weight of the drilling tools needed to tap the deeper sands. (Courtesy Cities Service Oil Company.)

Three Sands had no mayor, no city council, nor any other local government. With no organized fire department, except workers provided by the oil companies, and because of the field's output of light crude and high gas production, fires were constant dangers. One fire took five hundred men and nearly one hundred teams of horses and mules to extinguish. Oil field workers using shovels to kill any burning rats that ran from beneath the tanks. The rats, which often nested beneath the tanks, would catch fire and run under other storage tanks, thereby spreading the fires. The clouds of black smoke could be seen for miles and as many as three thousand sightseers stood around watching the flames. (Courtesy American Petroleum Institute.)

The Wentz Oil Corporation built a huge natural gasoline plant in Three Sands during the heyday of the field's outpouring of crude. The plant was located a little less than one mile east of the junction of Tonkawa's Main Street with the section line separating Kay and Noble counties. The large tin building directly behind the word "CORP" on the rooftop still stands. (Courtesy Marland Mansion.)

Most of the thousands of wells drilled during the heyday of the Three Sands oil boom have been cleaned up in an extensive remediation project overseen by the Oklahoma Energy Resources Board. This is one of the few, of what once was thousands, of well heads remaining. (Author's personal collection.)

The open prairie of the Three Sands Field provided little protection from the bitter north winds of winter. In this winter scene of the field, the steam escaping from the boilers used to power drilling operations blanket the rigs. Workers on the rig in the center of the photograph have built a windbreak of boards around the floor of the rig to make it warmer. The owner of the shotgun house in the lower foreground has replaced the glass in his windows with boards to help keep in the heat from the one wooden stove. Note the stovepipe extending above the roof. (Courtesy Western History Collections, University of Oklahoma Library.)

Located on the Kay County-Osage County border, the Burbank Field was discovered by the Marland Oil Company in 1920. It was one of the richest fields ever discovered in the United States, and by 1949 it ranked 21st among America's oil fields in total production. In 1924, Marland Oil Company paid $1,900,000 for a 160-acre lease 1.5 miles east of the Kay-Osage county line. (Courtesy Phillips Petroleum Company.)

Phillips Petroleum Company's natural gasoline plant was located on the extreme western edge of the Burbank Field. Because company officials wanted to keep their workers away from the vice and violence of the boom towns, Phillips built houses for the plant's employees. The houses can be seen in the upper right. Stretched along the road in the background are a number of tents—hence the name "Ragtown" written on the photograph. (Courtesy Phillips Petroleum Company.)

26

Lew Wentz (left) and William G. Skelly are standing on the runway of Spartan Aviation in Tulsa during World War II. Skelly formed Skelly Oil Company, with a capitalization of $15,000,000, on October 2, 1919—just in time for the discovery of the Burbank Field. He played a major role in the early development of the Tulsa-based Skelly Oil Company, which was eventually acquired by J. Paul Getty. (Courtesy Marland's Grand Home.)

Workers, pictured here, are completing Phillips Petroleum Company's huge natural gasoline plant in eastern Kay County. Many of the buildings had already been completed by the time this photograph was taken. Others were still in progress. Note the workers in the foreground pushing wheelbarrows up and down wooden planks leading from the cement mixer to where the foundation was being poured. (Courtesy Phillips Petroleum Company.)

27

Company dignitaries view a gusher in the Burbank Field along the Kay-Osage county line. Phillips Petroleum Company was a major developer of the field. The huge Phillips Petroleum Company natural gas plant in Kay County was connected to Burbank's wells by pipeline. Frank Phillips, head of Phillips Petroleum, is standing fourth from the right. Sixth from the right is Frank's son, John Phillips. F.E. Rice, head of Phillips Petroleum's Gasoline Division is second from right. (Courtesy Phillips Petroleum Company.)

Although located mostly in Osage County, the prolific Burbank Field overlapped into extreme eastern Kay County. On the right is a series of company houses for the plant's workers. It was company policy to provide housing for workers to keep them away from the distractions of the rowdy oil boom towns. Note the oil derricks marching east toward the heart of the Burbank Field. (Courtesy Phillips Petroleum Company.)

Workers are preparing to pour concrete for a floor for an extension to the machine shop at Phillips Petroleum Company's natural gasoline plant in the Burbank Field. Note the saddled mule between the truck in the upper center and the man carrying a length of reinforcement bar. For oilmen in the rugged terrain of eastern Kay County, mules and horses often provided the most reliable means of transportation. (Courtesy Phillips Petroleum Company.)

A row of company houses are still under construction at the Phillips Petroleum Company's natural gasoline plant in eastern Kay County in the Burbank Field. The house on the left has been completed. On the right, workers are just completing the framing, while the three houses in-between are in various stages of construction. The houses were built in assembly line fashion. (Courtesy Phillips Petroleum Company.)

Producers and Refiners Corporation was one of the major developers of the Kay County oil fields. Pictured here is their warehouse in the Burbank Field, just to the east of the Kay-Osage county line. Note the men on the left of the photograph wearing the oil-covered clothes and hard hats. Apparently, they have been working to bring a runaway gusher under control. (Courtesy Allen Muchmore.)

Two

THE BOOM TOWNS

During the first three decades of the 20th century, the lure of vast oil fortunes played a major role in the transformation of many of Kay County's quiet, farming communities into expanding, bustling oil boom towns. There were three types of oil boom towns in Kay County. Those such as Three Sands, Murray, Four Way, Kanolka, Hatchville, East Side, Foster City, Riverview, Blue Ridge, and Smackover were a direct result of a new find and owed their existence to the discovery of oil. Others, such as Blackwell, Kaw City, and Tonkawa had been agricultural communities before being swept up in the mad rush for oil. Still others, such as Ponca City or Newkirk, the county seat, were established commercial centers prior to the oil boom.

One thing they had in common, however, was a rapid influx of men and money once a nearby strike had been made. Their populations literally exploded as thousands of prospectors, promoters, scouts, gamblers, prostitutes, con men, scalpers, bootleggers, roughnecks, and others rushed to the new fields.

The boom town atmosphere produced scenes reminiscent of the Wild West. "Two-Ton Tilly" and "Three Sands Blanche" maintained boarding houses in Three Sands. Prostitutes plied their trade openly. John "Two Gun" Middleton and George "Three Finger" Miller shot it out with Jackson "Chief" Burns in front of the Blue Front Café. Middleton and Miller were killed and Burns was acquitted for self-defense.

Eventually, the boomtown era passed. Many of the communities retained their oil-based economies. Others returned to their quiet rural lifestyle, while yet others disappeared as the workers rushed to the next strike.

This is an early view of the Marland Refining Company complex in south Ponca City. On the left are some of the oil storage tanks that eventually held more than one million barrels of oil. Note the horse on the left. Marland built the refinery on an area that originally contained cattle pens where livestock were herded to be shipped to market by railroad. (Courtesy Marland Mansion.)

Lew Wentz, shown here with three young ladies, never married. His generosity for Kay County included spending $200,000 for a camp for the Ponca City Boy Scouts, establishment of a student loan program at the University of Oklahoma and Oklahoma State University, medical care for crippled children, and many other charitable programs. It was Wentz who supplied the funds for the erection of the Pioneer Woman Statue after E.W. Marland lost his fortune. (Courtesy Marland's Grand Home.)

Seven of E.W. Marland's first eight wells in the Ponca City Field were gassers. The gas was quickly piped to nearby communities for light and heat. The cheap supply of natural gas fueled operations of the United Sash and Door Company, seen here in 1913. The open flames used to manufacture glass resulted in extremely high temperatures in the sheet iron building. Note the large number of openings in the walls and roof. (Courtesy Pioneer Woman Statue.)

The Lake Park Refinery in Ponca City was located about where the Pioneer Woman Statue now stands. Note the diving board and three men swimming in the lake in the foreground. When E.W. Marland built his home on Grand Avenue in 1916, the refinery was located to the north where he later built a nine-hole golf course. Marland eventually purchased the refinery and tore it down as part of his landscaping for the Marland Mansion. (Courtesy Pioneer Woman Museum.)

Employees of the Ponca City Post Office posed for this photograph in 1912. Chloe Van Winkle is the general delivery clerk in the cage. The others are the post office's rural mail carriers. From left to right on the left side of the cage are Jim Gravett, Chat Hartshorne, and Jim Hooser; on the right side of the cage are Toad Action, Otis Bendure, and Fred Kirby. Note the mud on the floor and on the mail carriers' shoes and clothes. Although the Ponca City Post Office served a large number of rural residents prior to 1910, the discovery of oil touched off a rush for riches that brought thousands of workers into the county, greatly adding to the amount of mail passing through the post office. When the boom started, Ponca City's population was 2,500. Within a few years it was 15,000. (Courtesy Pioneer Woman Museum.)

Armistice Day, November 11, 1920, found Ponca City's Grand Avenue draped in patriotic banners. Two oil field workers in oil-stained clothing are crossing the street, while two boys riding their bicycles pass to the left. The automobiles are parked in front of the Murray Theater and W.K. Van Winkle's clothing store. (Courtesy Top of Oklahoma Museum.)

Notice the snow on the ground in this winter scene of the Globe Oil and Refinery Company at Blackwell. Blackwell and Ponca City were the two refining centers in Kay County. Because Blackwell was a major railroad junction, refineries could ship oil and refinery products throughout the county from the community. The tank in the foreground is surrounded by a dike to prevent the escape of overflowing or burning oil. (Courtesy Top of Oklahoma Museum.)

Because its railroad connections allowed the easy shipment of zinc from the Tri-State Mining District in eastern Oklahoma to Blackwell, where the smelter owners could find a plentiful and cheap supply of natural gas, Blackwell became a major zinc manufacturing community. The huge smokestack of the Blackwell Zinc Company, shown here, dominated the city's skyline from 1916 until 1975, when it was dismantled. (Courtesy Top of Oklahoma Museum.)

Just after the discovery of the Three Sands Oil Field, the boom town there began taking shape. The long building on the left is a rooming house, catering to oil field workers, according to the sign on the front. The rooming house had 11 rooms on each side of a long hallway running down the center. Note the path leading from the back of the rooming house to the two-hole privy. (Courtesy Top of Oklahoma Museum.)

Beginning in the spring of 1923, thousands of workers and camp followers flocked to the strike at Three Sands. The population of the community reached an estimated 10,000 with another 15,000 in the surrounding area. At first there was nothing but tents, dugouts and shacks for living accommodations. To provide better living conditions for their workers and to help keep them away from the multitude of gamblers, prostitutes, bootleggers and other undesirables who rushed to Three Sands, most major oil field companies built their own camps. The houses were structured according to company hierarchy. In the upper left are the more elaborate structures used for offices and visiting executives. In the foreground are four-room houses with porches for mid-level workers. Between the two are rows of flat-topped shotgun houses for ordinary workers. Notice that each house has an accompanying outdoor privy. (Courtesy Getty Refining and Marketing Company.)

Gay's Boarding House at Three Sands was typical of businesses feeding the thousands of oil field workers rushing to the strike. A customer is standing in front of the wood-floored porch of the business. A wooden plank has been laid across the open ditch beside the street. In the background are several shotgun houses with washing hanging on clotheslines strung between the houses and the outhouses behind them. (Courtesy Top of Oklahoma Museum.)

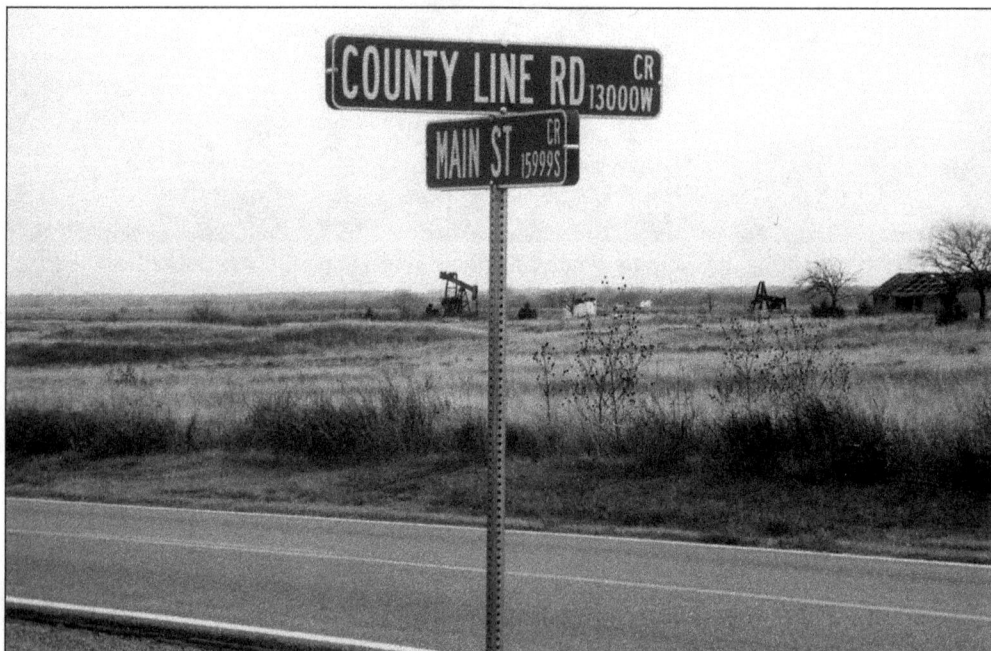

Three Sands was located near this intersection of Countyline Road, the border between Kay and Noble counties, and Main Street, which ran six miles from Tonkawa to Three Sands. A single building is all that stands of the once bustling oil boom town of Three Sands, the onetime home to tens of thousands of oil field workers. (Author's personal collection.)

The Atchison, Topeka, and Santa Fe Railroad Depot at Tonkawa now stands abandoned. The Santa Fe reached Tonkawa in 1899. As the gateway for the rush for black gold, an average of 800 railroad car loads of oil field supplies were shipped in and 120 tank cars of crude shipped out each month. (Author's personal collection.)

Smackover was located south of Tonkawa along the banks of the Salt Fork of the Arkansas River. It was said that every other building in Smackover was a saloon and those in between were brothels. In July of 1923, the Salt Fork flooded, covering Smackover with 10 feet of water and washing away many of the business. On the right of this photograph is Steve's Café, which survived the flood. (Courtesy McCarter Museum of Tonkawa History.)

Kay County's first courthouse opened in 1894, but was destroyed by fire on March 4, 1897. Another wood framed structure was hurriedly constructed and opened in the fall of 1897. Construction of a new courthouse was approved on August 1, 1922, but work did not begin until July, 1925. Hundreds attended the dedication of the new courthouse on October 26, 1926. The old wood frame one was sold at public auction for $750. (Courtesy Newkirk Community Historical Society.)

Like many other communities in the 1920s, Newkirk citizens were attracted to the Ku Klux Klan, which promoted law and order. In this parade, members of the women's auxiliary of the Klan (note the shoes of the marchers) are preparing to parade through the streets behind a criminal dressed in prison stripes. The Klan often took it upon themselves to end the worst of the vice and violence in the boom towns. (Courtesy Karen Dye.)

The Kay County Courthouse is in the lower left of this view of Seventh Street between Main Street on the right, and Maple Avenue on the left. The two-story building at the corner of Seventh and Maple is the Park Hotel, which catered to the many salesmen who visited Newkirk. Prostitutes could often be seen making their way along the alley between the Park Hotel and the Endicott Hotel, which was just around the corner. (Courtesy Newkirk Community Historical Society.)

The W.T. Conklin Grain Company elevator in Kaw City was beside the railroad depot. Kaw City was located on the Atchison, Topeka, and Santa Fe's mainline north-south rail line. W.T. Conklin, along with his brother M.C., also owned a hardware store in the community. (Courtesy Oklahoma Heritage Association.)

The famous Clubb Hotel in Kaw City was built by I.M. Clubb. His wife, Laura Abigail Clubb, was a patron of the arts and used the family's oil money to acquire one of the largest privately owned art collections in America. Many of the pieces in her collection decorated the lobby of the hotel. Much of her collection was later donated to the Philbrook Art Museum in Tulsa. (Courtesy Newkirk Community Historical Society.)

The flood of June 11, 1923, covered downtown Kaw City with water from the nearby Arkansas River. In the center of the photograph is the Kandy-Land Store. At the left side is the Marland Oil Company service station. Drilling started about eight miles east of Kaw City in the Burbank Field in 1919, and the community soon was swamped with oil field workers rushing to the strike. (Courtesy Newkirk Community Historical Society.)

In the 1960s, the government decided to dam the Arkansas River to control flooding. It bought up the property and moved Kaw City to higher ground, two miles west of the original site. In 1966, work was started on the 17,040-acre Kaw Lake. Impoundment of water started in 1976, and the original townsite was swallowed by the rising waters. (Courtesy Fred Marvel, Oklahoma Department of Tourism and Recreation.)

Located on Pike's Peak Hill near Kaw City stands this striking sculpture, *Consultant of the South Wind*, by sculptor Todd Whipple. (Courtesy Fred Marvel, Oklahoma Department of Tourism and Recreation.)

The Kaw City Museum keeps the past alive with its treasure trove of memorabilia and relics of times gone by. In this photograph are a few of the wringer washing machines housed in the museum. In the background items of women's clothing are displayed. (Courtesy Fred Marvel, Oklahoma Department of Tourism and Recreation.)

The Oil Field Short Line Railroad depot, pictured here on December 24, 1916, was located at the south end of Dilworth's Main Street. It was a subsidiary of the St. Louis and San Francisco Railroad and ran between the Frisco's mainline at Clifford and Dilworth. Passengers and freight headed for the oil wells in northern Kay County were switched to the Short Line at Clifford and hauled to Dilworth. (Courtesy Newkirk Community Historical Society.)

Typical of the oil boom towns, Burbank was filled with gamblers, bootleggers and other unsavory characters. Once, when the local prohibition agent instituted a crackdown of illegal saloons, local bootleggers persuaded a corrupt local lawman to "knock him off." The lawman and his girlfriend ambushed the agent. In the shoot-out the girlfriend was killed, the local lawman was shot three times and the prohibition agent wounded four times. He was back on duty in a few weeks. (Courtesy Jesse More.)

This is a double row of Phillips Petroleum Company's housing at Burbank. Paul Endicott, a young civil engineer with the company described his room at the company bunkhouse as a "clapboard shack...thrown together without insulation." During the frigid winter nights Endicott recalled the "wind howled down from the Osage Hills" and often filled the interior of the house with snow that had drifted through the cracks in the walls. (Courtesy Phillips Petroleum Company.)

Notice the maze of above-ground pipelines crisscrossing the prairie in the oil-rich Burbank Field in eastern Kay County, as seen from the edge of the Phillips Petroleum Company's gasoline plant. Gasoline from the plant was piped to DeNoya, where it could be loaded into railroad tank cars. The inhabitants of the two shotgun houses on the left have hung their laundry from a clothesline strung between the two structures. (Courtesy Phillips Petroleum Company.)

Company houses, such as this four-room Phillips Petroleum Company house at the company's natural gasoline plant, generally contained a living room, an opening through a screen door onto the front porch, two bedrooms, and a combination kitchen-dining room. Compared to the makeshift shotgun houses that predominated in most oil boom towns, such company-owned houses were luxurious. (Courtesy Phillips Petroleum Company.)

In this photograph carpenters are framing a four-room oil field house for workers at Phillips Petroleum Company's natural gasoline plant. The homes were built atop the ground on blocks of stone such as that stacked in the left foreground. Wooden piles supported the porch. There were no roads yet, however, a line of telephone poles stretched eastward toward the town of Burbank. (Courtesy Phillips Petroleum Company.)

Peck's Grocery Store in Braman, shown here, in northwestern Kay County, was five miles west of Dilworth and was on the Atchison, Topeka and Santa Fe Railroad. Many workers from the Dilworth Field bought their supplies at this store. The town was named for Dwight Braman, a railroad surveyor, who surveyed the town after local residents donated $3,000 to build a depot. (Courtesy Pioneer Woman Museum.)

This is outside a local blacksmith shop at Webb City, which was in Osage County two miles east of the Kay-Osage county line. Many residents of Webb City crossed into Kay County to work in the oil fields. The town quickly acquired the reputation of an oil boom town. Mrs. Don Conner, an early resident, recalled that "during the boom days, there was a man killed there almost every night." (Courtesy Don Conner.)

Dick Krohn (right) looking out of his garage in Whizbang in 1924, was a well-known businessman who served customers in the oil fields of eastern Kay County. He was often the target of hijackers who infested the Kay-Osage county border. Once his brother-in-law, Roy Cole, was kidnapped and held outside of Whizbang on a lonely county road by two hijackers. After Krohn refused to deliver the money to such a desolate spot, one of the hijackers became impatient and told his partner, "I guess he ain't never going to show up," and they let Cole go. In another attempt Bill Cooper, one of Krohn's friends, was kidnapped and forced to telephone Krohn to lure him out of town. Again Krohn refused and Cooper was freed. (Courtesy Dick Krohn.)

The townsite of Watchorn in Pawnee County was just east of the Three Sands Oil Field. Watchorn was named for Dr. Robert Watchorn of Redlands, California, and the founder of the Ardmore-based Watchorn Oil and Gas Company. Watchorn was one of the developers of the Three Sands Oil Field, controlling large amounts of oil and natural gas production with one of its leases producing six hundred barrels of high gravity oil daily. The Watchorn Field, in the southeast corner of the 101 Ranch, produced $10,000,000 worth of oil in ten years. Many oil field workers in southeastern Kay County lived in Watchorn. (Courtesy Marland's Grand Home.)

Three

BLACKWELL/101 RANCH

Prior to the Run of 1893, J.B. Lynee, William Whiting, F.T. Berkey, W.C. Robinson, and Ed L. Peckham—all businessmen from Winfield, Kansas—formed a townsite company. To secure acreage in the Cherokee Outlet, they arranged for Andrew J. Blackwell, an intermarried Cherokee, to secure allotments for three orphaned Cherokee children, George and Mary Palmer, and Mike Hendricks and his wife. Then three of the four 80-acre plots were sold to the townsite company. The other 80-acre plot was homesteaded by Frank Potts and sold to the developers for $1,050. The common name for the town during its early days was Blackwell Rock.

A mile to the south, the community of Parker was founded and became the chief competitor to Blackwell until the Chikaskia flooded and washed away most of Parker's buildings. Although Parker was revived as Chikaskia City, and then later as Kay City, Blackwell eventually swallowed up the settlement.

Granted a post office and originally called Parker, on December 1, 1893, Blackwell was the largest town in "K" County. By 1898, the St. Louis and San Francisco; Atchison, Topeka, and Santa Fe; and Hutchison and Southern railroads had built to Blackwell. Founded in 1899, Blackwell's Oklahoma Baptist College began holding classes in 1901, and by 1902 the community boasted seven saloons and an Anheiser-Bush brewery.

In 1902, several large natural gas wells were completed around Blackwell and the community boomed. In addition to the oil and gas business several other industries attracted by the cheap supply of natural gas located in the community. The largest of these was the Blackwell Zinc Company.

The flat prairie land north of Blackwell along the Chikaskia River and its tributaries was the heart of the Blackwell Field opened by E.W. Marland in 1914. Note the upright storage tank in the upper left. It is surrounded by a dike to contain burning oil should the tank catch fire. (Courtesy Top of Oklahoma Museum.)

The house and barn in the upper right belong to J.L. Welch. Welch owned some of the most productive acreage in the Blackwell Field. Note the oil-soaked drilling well, the oil covered ground around the well, and the oil filled pit. Obviously this well blew in as a gusher, spewing oil. (Courtesy Top of Oklahoma Museum.)

The sharpshooters of the 101 Ranch Wild West Show, shown here standing on Cowboy Hill on the ranch, from left to right, are George Eagle, son of White Eagle; Stark Lee; Ponca Chief White Eagle, holding the rifle on his hip; and W.S. Prettyman, pioneer photographer. After touring Kay County to locate potential oil well locations, E.W. Marland found a promising site—a hill on the Willie-Cries-for-War allotment on the 101 Ranch Lease. Unfortunately, the same hill was a traditional burial site for the Ponca Indians. The Indians were hesitant to allow Marland to drill, so he appealed to George Miller who convinced White Eagle to allow the well to be drilled. However, White Eagle warned Marland that the drilling on the hill would make "bad medicine," not only for White Eagle and the Poncas, but for Marland as well. This was the basis for the famous Marland curse. (Courtesy Top of Oklahoma Museum.)

The owners of the 101 Ranch in Kay County are, from left to right, Zach T. Miller, J.C. Miller, and George L. Miller. Between 1927 and 1929, the 101 Ranch's operations, including its oil production, totaled more than $3,000,000. However, Joe Miller died in 1927 and George in 1929. Coupled with the collapse of the oil boom in 1929, the Ranch fell on hard times and much of its holdings were sold to pay creditors. (Courtesy Oklahoma Heritage Association.)

Zack Miller (left) is shown here with George Star (center) and Obie Little Standing Buffalo (right). In 1916, Zack was in Texas to purchase mules when a battle broke out between Mexican Federales and rebels across the Rio Grande. When the Federales' wagon train, containing enough wagons, stock, machine guns and other supplies to equip five thousand troops, fled north of the river, Zack bought it for $40,000 in gold. (Courtesy Top of Oklahoma Museum.)

When the 101 Ranch and Wild West Show fell on hard times during the Great Depression, forcing Zack to sell off most of the animals and equipment, he barricaded himself in the famous White House Mansion and threatened to shoot court officials attempting to liquidate the properties. Creditors agreed to a two-year moratorium, but Zack was unable to reverse his plight and the land was sold and most of the ranch buildings torn down. (Courtesy Oklahoma Heritage Association.)

White Eagle was chief of the Ponca Tribe when they first arrived in Kay County in 1876–1877, and was the last war chief of the Poncas. He died February 3, 1914, at age 78. Afterward, the Miller brothers built a series of traditional Ponca signal mounds about 15 miles apart on the 101 Ranch. On one mound, a white stone eagle was placed on a pillar to honor Chief White Eagle. (Courtesy Pioneer Woman Museum.)

55

In 1923, the Salt Fork of the Arkansas flooded, and inundated the front yard of the White House of the 101 Ranch. Jack Baskin used his boat to rescue residents and take them to higher ground. Note the dog in the center of the boat and the man wearing a cowboy hat and dressed in a bathing suit standing on the front porch. (Courtesy Marland's Grand Home.)

The Poncas, originally from Nebraska and South Dakota, were moved to a reservation in present-day southeastern Kay and northeast Noble counties in 1876–1878, and became known as the Hot Country Ponca. In 1880, the Ponca Indian Boarding School was opened at the Ponca Agency in extreme southeastern Kay County. It continued operation until 1919. (Courtesy Pioneer Woman Museum.)

The performers for the first 101 Ranch Wild West Roundup lined up for a mile-long procession. The Miller Brothers—Zack, George, and Joe—organized the first roundup in June of 1905. Thirty trains brought spectators to the Ponca City railroad depot. From the depot, an estimated 65,000 people attended the first show. (Courtesy Top of Oklahoma Museum.)

Although he shunned extravagance and display, Lew Wentz's racy convertible, seen here, was a common site in Kay County. Wentz first met E.W. Marland when Marland was acquiring oil leases for the 101 Ranch Oil Company, and he followed Marland's example in acquiring Kay County oil leases. (Courtesy Marland's Grand Home.)

In this photograph of Blackwell's Main Street, taken on May 12, 1894, the street is lined with wagons. At this time the railroads had not yet reached Blackwell, and local businesses were dependent on teams and freight wagons to haul supplies from Kildare. Passengers either caught a ride on the freight wagons or the Ferguson Brothers Stage Line from Kildare to Blackwell. (Courtesy Top of Oklahoma Museum.)

Although Newkirk had been designated the seat of Kay County in 1894, much of the area's official business was handled at Blackwell's federal courthouse, seen here. Shortly after statehood, petitions were circulated to relocate the seat to either Blackwell or Ponca City. Blackwell won the initial election in 1908, but because it did not receive a majority of votes it was forced into a runoff election with Newkirk, and lost by 49 votes. (Courtesy Oklahoma Heritage Association.)

The Blackwell Fire Department poses in front of the City Hall built in 1909. The City Hall also housed the Police Department. Although Blackwell was a well-established community prior to the discovery of oil nearby, it did undergo a boom town period. In 1907, prior to prohibition, Blackwell contained seven saloons and an Anheiser-Busch brewery. (Courtesy Top of Oklahoma Museum.)

Founded by the Baptist General Convention in 1899, classes at the Oklahoma State Baptist College in Blackwell started on September 4, 1902, and by 1911 the school had 208 students. Two years later, in 1913, the Baptist General Convention of Oklahoma closed it and moved its facilities to Shawnee. Afterward, the building was converted into the first osteopathic hospital in Oklahoma. (Courtesy Top of Oklahoma Museum.)

Although Blackwell had a brickyard in operation within 45 days of the Run of September 16, 1893, which opened the region to settlement, it was many years before all of the community's streets were paved with brick. The Sanitarium Bus Line, shown here, negotiated the mud-clogged streets during rainy weather. (Courtesy Top of Oklahoma Museum.)

This is the Oklahoma Business College at Blackwell's Class of 1911 posing for their class picture. The student on the right is operating the latest modern typewriter for the period. The Kay County oil boom resulted in a huge demand for office personnel as oil companies rushed to open offices in the region. (Courtesy Pioneer Woman Museum.)

Art Hess poses for a photograph in his sulky in front of the new Blackwell City Hall in 1909. The sulky was considered a "gentleman's vehicle," and Hess is dressed the part. (Courtesy Top of Oklahoma Museum.)

Mobile Oil Company was another major energy concern in Kay County. This is the Mobile Oil Company's service station in Blackwell in the 1920s. The amount of gasoline purchased was pumped into the glass container on top of the pumps, and then emptied into the automobile through a gravity-fed hose. A sign identifying the "Ladies Restroom" can be seen on the left of the station. (Courtesy Top of Oklahoma Museum.)

A young Lewis Haines "Lew" Wentz arrived in Ponca City in 1911, three years after E.W. Marland. Operating with limited financial resources, Wentz managed to get his start during the Blackwell oil boom and by the mid-1920s controlled production amounting to 20,000 barrels of oil daily in the Blackwell and Three Sands fields. (Courtesy Marland's Grand Home.)

Members of the Blackwell Fire Department pose with their 50-gallon two-horse wagon in 1909, the same year the department was organized with Jim Taplin as chief. The horses are named Mac and Tim. Taplin, a former school teacher, organized one of the state's first training schools for firefighters and authored *The Essentials of Firemanship.* (Courtesy Top of Oklahoma Museum.)

Some natural gas wells in the Blackwell Field had an initial flow of 200,000,000 cubic feet per day. The plentiful supply of natural gas attracted a multitude of new businesses, searching for a cheap supply of fuel. Among them were several glass companies such as the Oklahoma Bottle and Glass Factory, seen in this photograph. (Courtesy Top of Oklahoma Museum.)

The B & B Oil Company's Phillips 66 gasoline station was owned by Bill Krautzer (left) and Bryan Gates in Blackwell. Phillips Petroleum Company was one of the major developers of the oil resources in Kay County and early on expanded its Phillips 66 brands into the area. (Courtesy Top of Oklahoma Museum.)

Mrs. Mable C. Orr of Blackwell was one of the few women drilling contractors active in the state's oil fields in the 1920s. She was a partner of Dunham & Orr, which drilled several wells in the Braman and Blackwell Fields. (Courtesy Mrs. Claude V. Barrow.)

The Blackwell Zinc Company's plant was the largest multi-condenser, horizon retort type zinc smelter in the world at one time. During its heyday the smelter employed between seven hundred and eight hundred workers. When the oil boom era passed, the zinc smelter provided a mainstay to Blackwell's economy until it was closed in 1974. (Courtesy Top of Oklahoma Museum.)

This is part of the crew of the number three furnace at the Blackwell Zinc Company's plant. They are, from left to right, as follows: (front row) Carl Zeik, Henry Rick, Jack Ryan, George Atteberry, Carl Small, "Hook" Ellis, Tommy Glaze, Ed Coleman, Whitey Mitchell, and Julius Salima; (back row) Ed Blower, Clyde Bass, Carl Box, Otis Arnold, and Carl Ballett. Herman Meyers is standing behind the post on the back row. (Courtesy Top of Oklahoma Museum.)

The Blackwell Hospital, at 720 West College Avenue, served the community and surrounding oil fields until 1955. Seriously injured oil field workers were rushed to the hospital, which had a complete—and for the times, modern—surgery suite. (Courtesy Top of Oklahoma Museum.)

Now housing the Top of Oklahoma Historical Society's Cherokee Outlet Museum, Blackwell's Electric Park Pavilion was designed by architect W.L. McAltee. Located at 300 South Main Street, construction of the pavilion began in 1912. Officially opened on Easter Sunday, 1913, the brick and stucco structure features an 80-by-140 foot pavilion, with a 20-foot ceiling and four columns. Its Romanesque design features a ribbed dome and half moon arches above each window. Electric lights outline the dome, windows, and the outside flag poles. The exterior grounds are landscaped with plants, strolling paths, fishponds, lighted fountains, and sculptures. (Courtesy Top of Oklahoma Museum.)

Four

NEWKIRK/DILWORTH

When the Cherokee Outlet was thrown open to homesteaders on September 16, 1893, present-day Kay County was temporarily designated "K" County, Oklahoma Territory. At the time of the run, Newkirk was designated the county seat.

Originally, the post office at Newkirk was named Santa Fe, and the townsite called Lamereux; but a vote was taken to change the town's name to Santa Fe. However, the railroad refused to accept the name Santa Fe, so it was changed again—this time to Newkirk. A wood frame courthouse was built in 1894, but burned in March of 1897. In 1901, a disastrous fire destroyed an entire block on the east side of Newkirk's Main Street. By 1910, most of the downtown area had been rebuilt in limestone.

Newkirk continued its slow, steady growth as an agriculture center until the opening of Kay County's rich oil and natural gas deposits. As the county seat, Newkirk was the center of leasing activity and a Mecca for oil scouts and promoters flocking to the strikes.

Located ten miles northwest of Newkirk, Dilworth was granted a post office on March 17, 1917. Development of the town started after the discovery of the Dilworth Oil Field in 1911, and by the middle of the decade it was a thriving community.

Most of the businesses were typical wooden clapboard structures with sheet iron roofs. Such buildings quickly dried out in the hot dry summers and became tinderboxes. On April 26, 1926, Dilworth's business district was razed by fire. All but four of the town's businesses were destroyed. It was the end of the once thriving boom town. On March 30, 1929, the Dilworth Post Office closed.

Dilworth was platted by Joe A. Frates, an official with the St. Louis and San Francisco Railroad. To ensure the town's growth, Frates succeeded in having a spur line—known as the Oil Field Short Line Railway—built from the main line at Clifford about seven miles to the southeast. There was no turnaround for the engine at Dilworth, so after arriving the train backed up to Clifford. (Courtesy Top of Oklahoma Museum.)

Judging by the large number of wagons on the street, this photograph of Newkirk's business district was probably taken on a Saturday, when most farmers visited town to do their week's shopping. Note the chain stretched between the posts for customers to tie their horses. The sign on the pole advertises the coming of Gentry's "Famous Dog and Pony Show." (Courtesy Newkirk Community Historical Society.)

The disastrous fire of April 26, 1926, which burned all but four of Dilworth's businesses, started in the power room of the Electric Theater, seen on the right. The streets are still dirt in this photograph, but most businessmen have built wooden boardwalks in front of their establishments to keep customers out of the mud when it rained. (Courtesy Newkirk Community Historical Society.)

The building in the center of the photograph with pillars and arched entryways is the First National Bank of Newkirk. Originally organized as the Kay County State Bank on October 12, 1893, by P.W. Smith, it was the oldest bank in the community. Two doors down to the right is the State Guarantee Bank, which was organized by J.S. Eastman and P.S. Mason in 1909. (Courtesy Newkirk Community Historical Society.)

Newkirk has the largest number of cut limestone buildings in the state. Note the pole rig used to haul cut limestone blocks to the top of the building under construction on the right of the photograph. This is the intersection of Seventh Street and Main Street in downtown Newkirk. The area around Newkirk was one of two places in Oklahoma Territory that contained construction-quality limestone. (Courtesy Karen Dye.)

The original Santa Fe Railroad Depot at Newkirk, shown in this photograph, was replaced in 1916 by a larger brick building to handle the increased traffic resulting partially from the oil rush to Kay County. Newkirk was designated county seat for "K" County following the opening of the Cherokee Outlet to homesteaders in 1893. Old Kirk was a small hay station on the St. Louis and San Francisco Railroad. Newkirk was two miles to the south. (Courtesy Newkirk Community Historical Society.)

Newkirk's Concert Band often played in the bandstand on the courthouse square. This photograph was taken on the steps of the Newkirk High School, which was built in 1915. Among the band members were Harold Kelly, Virgil Jones, Jim Hamlin, Mancel Lane, Scott Westmore, George Wilson, Bill George, Munson Hamlin, Frank Westmore, Mert Hoefer, Lawrence Hoefer, Hiram Metz, Fred Zieger, and Henry Garside. (Courtesy Newkirk Community Historical Society.)

Harve Christy's Horse and Mule Market, pictured in 1918, was located on South Main Street across the street from the Newkirk High School. Although Christy specialized in farm animals, the onset of the Kay County oil boom greatly increased the demand for horses and mules in the surrounding oil fields. (Courtesy Newkirk Community Historical Society.)

Although the original plans for the Oil Field Short Line Railroad between the St. Louis and San Francisco's mainline at Clifford and Dilworth called for a turnaround at Dilworth, it was never built. Thus the train pulled the cars to Dilworth then backed up the four miles to Crawford. In this photograph the viewer is looking north toward downtown Dilworth. The engine is parked at the south end of Main Street. (Courtesy Newkirk Community Historical Society.)

Looking southwest toward the Kay County Courthouse from Newkirk's Co-op Block on August 24, 1897, the large building in the upper left is the second Kay County Courthouse that had just been completed. The first courthouse burned on March 4, 1897. When the third courthouse was completed in 1926, the second courthouse was sold for $750 at public auction. (Courtesy Newkirk Community Historical Society.)

In November of 1910, the entire block on the east side of Newkirk's Main Street between Sixth and Seventh Streets was destroyed by fire. Seven saloons, two dry goods stores, a barbershop, grocery store, restaurant, confectionery, and several other businesses were destroyed. Note the piles of merchandise in the street. With no community water system to fight the fire, the flames spread quickly and businessmen hurriedly carried what they could to safety. (Courtesy Newkirk Community Historical Society.)

In this photograph, probably taken from the water tower on the courthouse square in Newkirk, the view is looking west across Maple Avenue. In the lower left is Ada Garside's Photo Gallery. In the upper left is the Methodist Church. The church was originally the Salvation Army Hall that the congregation purchased and moved to the site in 1896. (Courtesy Newkirk Community Historical Society.)

This is the Joseph E. Hancock Dray and Transfer Company at Newkirk as it looked in 1908. Pictured here, from left to right, are the following: (front row) Joseph E. Hancock, Fred C. Neitert, G.L. Milam, and U.S. Curry; (second row, seated on the wagons) Carrol E. Hunt, Hancock's brother-in-law, Leon Darling, Carl Parkins, and Clint Ponc. The company delivered merchandise throughout the oil fields of northern Kay County. (Courtesy Karen Dye.)

When Newkirk was first established following the Run of 1893, Hank Paris delivered the mail by wagon until the local post office was opened in January of 1894. Pictured inside the post office is John Schramm, seated on the left. Standing behind him is Art Bunnell, and to the right of Bunnell is Muncie Hamlie. Art Leighty is in the near right portion of the picture. (Courtesy Karen Dye.)

74

The Christenson well produced so much natural gas that it took the crew several days to bring it under control. The Dilworth and Blackwell fields produced huge quantities of natural gas and the wells often blew open for several days. Bringing wild natural gas wells under control was dangerous work because the slightest spark could ignite spewing gas. Note the white cloud of escaping natural gas to the right of the drilling rig. (Courtesy Karen Dye.)

A huge crowd of onlookers watch a burning gas well in the Dilworth Field. Dilworth had a huge production of natural gas, and often when the bits unexpectedly encountered high-pressure pockets of gas, the tools were thrown back up the hole by the gas and the flames in the well's boilers ignited the escaping gas. (Courtesy Newkirk Community Historical Society.)

The Farmers National Bank building on the west side of Newkirk's Main Street was organized on November 15, 1899, by A.S. Slosson, who served as president, and cashier J.H. Coleman. The Farmers National was a mainstay of northern Kay County's economy until it was absorbed by the Eastman National Bank in 1936, during the Great Depression. At the north end of the block the Endicott Hotel can be seen. (Courtesy Newkirk Community Historical Society.)

Newkirk's Eastman National Bank building at the corner of Seventh and Main Streets was founded by E.B. Eastman on October 3, 1893, as the Bank of Santa Fe. In 1908, a federal charter was acquired and its name changed to the Eastman National Bank. The cut limestone building with its distinctive windows was built by Neimiah Tubbs. As he was completing the building, Tubbs fell from the roof and broke both his legs. (Courtesy Newkirk Community Society.)

Pictured is Black Diamond, the famous trotting ostrich, and the four-wheel cart he pulled in races against horses at the Kay County Fair in Newkirk. Black Diamond won. (Courtesy Newkirk Community Historical Society.)

A group of the first automobiles in Newkirk were gathered for this photograph in front of Marion Stewart's home. Stewart owned the first automobile in the community, the Oldsmobile in the center of the photograph. The two vehicles on the outside are Franklin Steamers. (Courtesy Newkirk Community Historical Society.)

Owned and operated by John Welch and his two sons, James and Frank, the Welch Auto Company was the local Ford dealership in Newkirk. The opening of the Dilworth Oil Field greatly increased Welch's business as oil companies flocked to the area. The pickup on the left of this photograph belongs to the Magnolia Oil Company, and to its left, beneath the tree, is a tank truck belonging to the Pirtle-Pittman Refining Company of Newkirk. (Courtesy Newkirk Community Historical Society.)

Dilworth boomed during Kay County's early oil rush. The dirt main street was lined by typical boom town businesses, such as the Hillsdale Rooming House, O.F. Graff Rooming House, the Star Rooming House, Keith and DeRossett Pool Hall, Bob and Babe Morrell's Pool Hall, and others. Its business district was a collection of hastily constructed structures, each with an outdoor privy. (Courtesy Allen Muchmore.)

Five

TONKAWA/THREE SANDS

Laid out on the homesteads of Eli V. Blake and William W. Gregory following the opening of the Cherokee Outlet, Tonkawa was granted a post office on March 9, 1894. It was not until late 1895 that a bridge across the Salt Fork of the Arkansas River allowed access to the rest of Kay County. However, it was the discovery of oil that caused Tonkawa to boom. With the opening of the nearby fields, the town's population jumped from less than two thousand in 1910 to nearly ten thousand during the 1920s. South Main Street became the center of the oil business.

Three Sands was a wide open oil boomtown, located on the line between southern Kay County and northern Noble County. Lawbreakers could escape the jurisdiction of the county sheriff by walking to the other side of Main Street. At its height Three Sands boasted two high schools, six grade schools, five gasoline plants, eleven boarding houses and a three-mile long wooden boardwalk.

With only two deputy sheriffs to patrol the estimated 8,000 to 15,000 inhabitants, the lawmen were quickly overwhelmed. In an effort to clean up the town, lawmen once rounded up three hundred prostitutes and ordered them aboard an outbound train headed for Kansas. Authorities planned to drop them off as the train made its way north, but the ladies would rush to windows in the passenger cars and expose their bare buttocks to local residents. Local lawmen refused to allow them off the train and most of the prostitutes ended up back in Three Sands.

This photograph is of the Sam McKee lease. McKee made the Run of 1893, and claimed a 160-acre homestead on which he and his wife raised nine children. In 1913, he leased his farm for ten cents an acre and for the next eight years drew 16 dollars a year in lease money. In 1921 Lew Wentz acquired the McKee lease and began drilling in the area. When oil was found on McKee's farm, his royalty jumped to $2,000,000 annually. Eventually, 69 wells were drilled on the McKee lease, with one well, the McKee No. 44, once being the most profitable well in the entire state. (Courtesy McCarter Museum of Tonkawa History.)

Tonkawa was named for the Tonkawa Indians, who were settled on the old Nez Perce Reservation in Kay County in 1885. Six years later, the Tonkawas accepted individual allotments and their surplus lands were opened to homesteaders in the Run of 1893. Many of the Tonkawas stayed on their allotments and during the oil boom could be seen in traditional dress along Tonkawa's streets. (Courtesy McCarter Museum of Tonkawa History.)

P.E. Rogers (center) operated several trucks hauling oil field equipment from supply houses in Tonkawa to the wells at Three Sands. Both the Oil Well Supply Company and National Supply Company warehouses were along the railroad right-of-way. Behind the truck, marked with a sign saying "Private Ground-Grain Only" is a small grain loading facility. Before the oil boom, Tonkawa's economy was based on the surrounding wheat fields. (Courtesy McCarter Museum of Tonkawa History.)

Originally built by the Methodists at 401 West Grand in Tonkawa, this building was sold to the local Catholic parish in 1908 and served the community's Catholic residents until 1926. In April of 1922, the Ku Klux Klan staged its first parade in Tonkawa. Although the Klan preached its goal was to rid Kay County of the vice and violence of the oil field boomtowns, Klan literature of the period was extremely anti-Catholic. (Courtesy Oklahoma Heritage Association.)

The Stricklen Hospital in Tonkawa was built by Dr. H.M. Stricklen to care for oil field workers injured in the Three Sands Field. The sounds from the nearby oil field—large exhaust pipes in the gasoline and pumping plants made a lot of noise—often made it impossible for patients to rest. The oil companies were eventually persuaded to muffle the exhaust so the patients could sleep. (Courtesy McCarter Museum of Tonkawa History.)

The Oil Well Supply Company warehouse in Tonkawa was the major supply company for oil field equipment for the Three Sands Field. Note the heavy chains on the rear mud-covered wheels of the truck. The unimproved dirt roads of the oil field made getting the equipment to the wells a challenge for drivers, especially in rainy weather. (Courtesy McCarter Museum of Tonkawa History.)

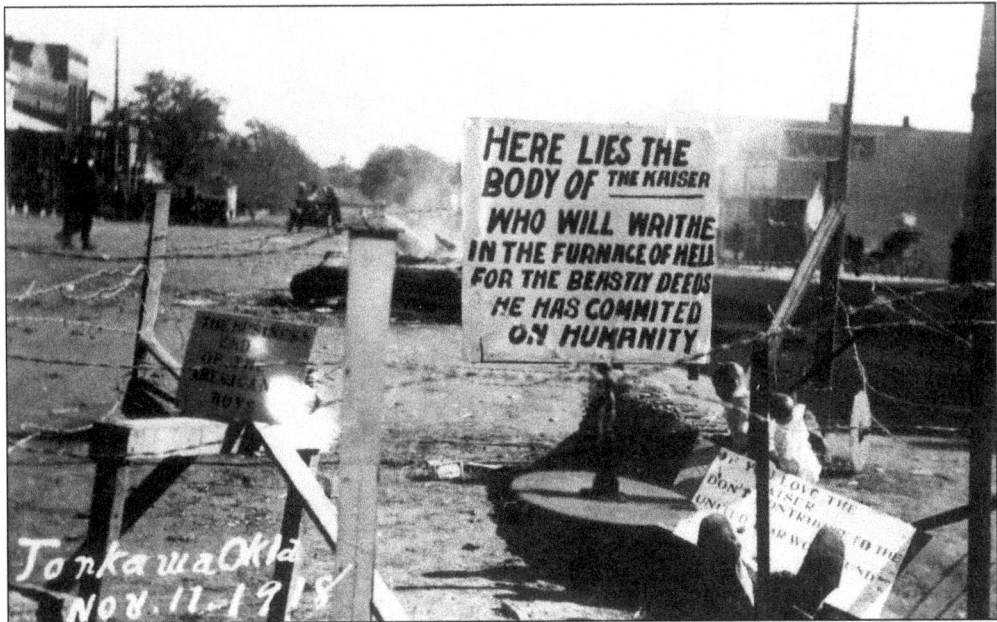

When World War I ended on Armistice Day, November 11, 1918, oil workers and other residents of Tonkawa gathered on the town's Main Street to burn the Kaiser in effigy. The sign on top of the Kaiser's effigy reads, "If You Love The Kaiser Don't Contribute to the United War World Fund." (Courtesy McCarter Museum of Tonkawa History.)

The date on the old Masonic Lodge building in downtown Tonkawa is 1900; however, the nine is backwards. Traditionally the Masons held their meetings on the second floor and rented out the bottom floor of their buildings to businesses. The Tonkawa Masonic Lodge was one of the leaders in the maintenance of law and order in the community during its oil boom town era. (Author's personal collection.)

This group of workers is standing in front of the National Supply Company warehouse in Tonkawa. Note that the truck, loaded with pipe destined for the Three Sands field, has had a wooden cab built over what was once the open driver's compartment to protect the driver from the elements. The truck is owned by P.E. Rogers, according to a sign above its door. (Courtesy McCarter Museum of Tonkawa History.)

Salt Fork River, Tonkawa, Okla.

Hasselwood & Sons, Publishers.

On the south bank of the Salt Fork of the Arkansas River, between Tonkawa and Three Sands, a tent city sprang up in 1922 as workers rushed to the wells along the Kay-Noble county line. The settlement, called Smackover, stretched for one thousand feet along the road. It disappeared when the Salt Fork flooded in June of 1923, washing away the "sin-filled" settlement under ten feet of water. (Courtesy Oklahoma Heritage Association.)

The bridge over the Arkansas River south of Tonkawa offered the shortest route between Tonkawa and Three Sands. This is the area where the settlement of Smackover was located. When the river flooded, the road was blocked and vehicles such as the Sanitary Bakery's delivery truck could not make their rounds. One of the buildings shown in this photograph is just starting to float downstream. (Courtesy McCarter Museum of Tonkawa History.)

In the upper left of this photograph is the C.C. Endicott Farm. By November of 1922, a small shack on the farm was selling sandwiches, ham and eggs, and coffee to oil field workers. This was the beginning of the boom town of Three Sands. The community was first called Comar, after the Comar Oil Company, but local merchants and oilmen later settled on the name of Three Sands. (Courtesy McCarter Museum of Tonkawa History.)

Tent structures, such as this one, characterized Three Sands. "Flop tents," one of which was operated by the Lee-Huckins Hotel in Oklahoma City, contained rows of cots often rented out to workers, with one worker crawling into a cot that was still warm from the previous occupant. One large circus tent housed a 16-table pool hall, a dance hall with a wooden floor, and a boarding house. (Courtesy McCarter Museum of Tonkawa History.)

Many of the early businessmen arriving in Three Sands lived either in the back of their establishments or in tents behind their business. Note the two tents behind these two businesses. Potable water for cooking and drinking was in short supply and was delivered by a water wagon that made its rounds among the boom town businesses. George Howerton once recalled that while just walking across the road to get a drink of water, a prostitute stopped him and asked $3.00 for her services. Eventually, a 250-gallon redwood water tank was built. When the water from the tank became so foul that no one would drink it, city officials climbed up to investigate and found a body floating in the water tank. (Courtesy McCarter Museum of Tonkawa History.)

This photograph of some lease houses in the Three Sands Field was taken as the field matured. The shotgun house on the right has had a room added to the side, and the house on the left has a garage in the back. Between the two houses is a storm cellar the residents apparently shared. The earlier wooden oil storage tanks have been replaced by steel tanks, and the scars of saltwater pits can be seen by the well sites. (Courtesy Allen Muchmore.)

This is the Wentz Oil Company's field office in the Three Sands Field. Lew Wentz, the founder, was a high school baseball coach in Pittsburgh, Pennsylvania, when he met John C. McCaskey, a millionaire sauerkraut king. McCaskey hired Wentz and sent him to Ponca City to oversee his oil properties. Wentz quickly formed his own company and by 1927 he was one of the six wealthiest men in America. (Courtesy Allen Muchmore.)

The main thoroughfare of Three Sands stretched for three miles. A wooden boardwalk lined both sides of the road. The wooden boardwalk can be seen on the left of this photograph. The man on the left has just passed a gasoline station (note the old-time hand-cranked pump next to the boardwalk) and is headed toward a barbershop and the American Café. The street became a muddy mire in the rain. (Courtesy McCarter Museum of Tonkawa History.)

These company houses of the Wentz Oil Company at Three Sands are surrounded by a fence and sidewalks and have indoor plumbing and trees planted in their yards. Such accommodations were necessary to get more highly skilled workers to come to Three Sands inasmuch as they did not want their families exposed to the vice and violence of the boom towns. Note the American flags flying in front of each house. (Courtesy McCarter Museum of Tonkawa History.)

Mother Smith's Boarding House, seen on the left, was typical of the living accommodations available in Three Sands. Note the unpaved street. During rainy weather the ruts were often up to the hubcaps of automobiles. As a result, teams of horses and mules became very valuable. Farmers would hire out their teams to pull automobiles out of the mud. Some farmers filled holes with water at night to increase their business. (Courtesy McCarter Museum of Tonkawa History.)

The crew of the Texas Worth Tool Company at Three Sands poses for a company photograph, c. 1930. C.F. Williams Sr. was the local manager. Ted Reiger is the third man from the right and Glenn McGovern is the fourth from the right. Notice the oil-stained clothes and sunburned foreheads. (Courtesy McCarter Museum of Tonkawa History.)

The Wentz Oil Company warehouse was surrounded by wells in the Three Sands Field. Lew Wentz, one of the early developers, was once offered $1,300,000 for the Sam McKee lease and turned it down. Eventually, McKee's farm proved to be the field's production center. Wentz made a $3,000,000 profit on one of the 68 wells drilled on the lease. (Courtesy Allen Muchmore.)

Not all of Three Sands was gambling dens, brothels, saloons, and dance halls. This is the Rhythm Band at the local elementary school. The huge influx of oil field money provided oil boom town schools with money that allowed them to offer programs unheard of in neighboring communities. (Courtesy McCarter Museum of Tonkawa History.)

The broadside on the right of the Cozy Theater's entrance in Three Sands advertises Lottie Pickard in *They Shall Pay*. The theater is typical boom town construction of wooden siding over a 2-by-4 frame. The roof is covered with tar paper. When sleeping accommodations became short, it was not unusual for local workers to pay to see a movie just so they could sleep in the seats. (Courtesy Western History Collections, University of Oklahoma Library.)

The Central Machine Tool & Supply Shop at Three Sands was across the road from the Hotel Foster. The nearest railroad depot was at Tonkawa, therefore all heavy equipment and supplies had to be hauled to the field on dirt roads connecting the two communities. At the height of the Three Sands boom an estimated eight thousand individuals lived in the town and another seven thousand in the nearby field. (Courtesy Top of Oklahoma Museum.)

Six

E. W. MARLAND

Born May 8, 1874, Ernest Whitworth Marland received a law degree from the University of Michigan in 1891. After graduation, Marland settled in Pittsburgh, working in a law office until he was 21, when he opened his own practice and later, an oil exploration company. In 1903, Marland married Mary Virginia Collins.

Shortly after losing millions of dollars in the Panic of 1907, Marland heard about the oil and gas possibilities on the 101 Ranch south of Ponca City. He arrived in Ponca City in 1908, and soon formed the 101 Ranch Gas Company with George Miller. In 1917, E.W. formed Marland Oil Co. and Marland Refining Co., and soon built an energy concern that controlled almost ten percent of the world's oil production.

E.W. and Virginia had no children. In 1912, George and Lydie Roberts, Virginia's sister's children, were brought to Ponca City to live with them. The Marlands legally adopted the two in 1916. Virginia died in 1926 after a long bout with cancer. Two years later, Marland took Lydie back to Pennsylvania, had her adoption annulled and married her.

In early 1928, Marland found his company $30,000,000 in debt to J.P. Morgan & Co. and within a year was forced to resign as president and was replaced by Dan Moran. In 1929, Marland Oil acquired Continental and became Continental Oil Company, later Conoco.

Marland turned to politics and was elected to Congress in 1932, and as Governor of Oklahoma in 1934. However, Marland's days as a millionaire were over, and in 1941 he sold the Marland Mansion, retaining ownership of approximately three acres and a few buildings on the grounds, where he lived until his death on October 3, 1941.

E.W. Marland is stretched on the grass in front of friends in 1906. Virginia, Marland's wife, is in the second row next to George Roberts, her nephew, whom the Marlands later adopted. John G. McCaskey, in the middle of the back row, became known as the "Sauerkraut King" after Marland arranged for a contract with the farmers of Dutchess County, New York, giving McCaskey an option for the annual cabbage crop. (Courtesy Marland Mansion.)

On November 5, 1903, Mary Virignia Collins, pictured here, married E.W. Marland in her Philadelphia, Pennsylvania home. Her father, Sam Collins Sr., was a local court stenographer. E.W. and Mary had no children, but in 1916 adopted her niece and nephew, Lydie and George Roberts. (Courtesy Marland Mansion.)

Mary Virginia Marland entertained numerous guests in the Marland family suite in Ponca City's Arcade Hotel, the family's home from 1908 until 1911. Although his fortunes improved after discovering natural gas in the Ponca City Field in 1910, until then Marland ate mulligan stew that he cooked at his well-site in an old can. Even so, he maintained his appearance, dressing in knickerbockers, a belted Norfolk jacket and spats. (Courtesy Marland Mansion.)

Lydie Marland, seen here in the plaid dress, celebrates her 14th birthday on April 7, 1914. Some of her attending friends, from left to right, are as follows: (front row) Marjorie Panton, Lydie Roberts, and Gwendolyn Moore; (back row) Ruth McDowell, Rose Soldina, Mary Hall, Jessie Scott, and Annie Lee Broaddos. (Courtesy Marland Mansion.)

More than $25,000,000 worth of oil was produced from Marland's original 160-acre Three Sands lease. Marland also held the lease to another 240 acres adjoining the original acreage. Needing money, Marland offered a one-half interest in the adjoining lease to Carter Oil Company for $1,000,000. The offer was declined because Carter Oil Company's geologists reported that they "couldn't see the field as being profitable." (Courtesy Pioneer Woman Museum.)

Marland's first mansion in Ponca City was on Grand Avenue. This view is from the backyard, looking from southeast to northwest. On the right is the east terrace. The Marland's bedroom occupied the east wing of the second floor, overlooking the formal gardens that measured 1,600 feet in length and 400 feet in width. The Marland family lived here for 12 years. (Courtesy Pioneer Woman Museum.)

These three fountains marked the east end of the formal gardens facing the terrace of Marland's home. The eight acres of formal gardens were patterned after the Gardens of Versailles. According to Sandy McDonald, the golf pro at the nine-hole golf course to the north of the home, the material and labor used to landscape the gardens and the golf course exceeded $1,000,000 in the first six years. (Courtesy Pioneer Woman Museum.)

Known as Marland's "Grand Home," this showplace was designed by Solomon Andrew Layton, renowned Oklahoma architect, and built in 1916. The mansion contains 22 rooms and 16,542 square feet of floor space on four levels. It originally included a central vacuuming system, automatic dishwasher and a three-car garage. Under the east terrace is one of the first indoor swimming pools in Oklahoma. (Courtesy Fred Marvel, Oklahoma Department of Tourism and Recreation.)

97

One of Lydie Marland's favorite pastimes was dancing. She and her friends often danced on the east terrace of the Marland home at 1000 East Grand Avenue. Lydie and her brother George were the children of Virginia Marland's sister. They came to live with E.W. and Virginia in 1912, and were legally adopted by the Marlands in 1916. (Courtesy Marland Mansion.)

Jo Davidson's statue of Lydie Marland was originally placed on the north lawn of the Marland Mansion, where E.W. could view it from the breakfast room. Years later, after the mansion had been sold to the Discalced Carmelite Fathers and E.W. had died, the monks requested Lydie remove the statue. She did so and had it broken up and buried. The pieces were recovered in 1993 and the statue restored. (Courtesy Marland Mansion.)

This is the first trainload of Marland gasoline to be shipped from the Marland Refinery facility in 1919. It contained 25 tank cars and was consigned to the Northern Oil Company in Bay City, Wisconsin. Other shipments had been made, but this was the first entire trainload. The company owned and operated 320 tank cars at this time. Conductor Sam Dennis is seen standing in the door of the caboose. (Courtesy Conoco, Inc.)

This 1922 photograph shows Marland with some of the men instrumental to his early success. They are, from left to right, P.B. Lowrance, Marland, W.H. McFadden, executive vice president of the Marland Oil Co., who helped underwrite the discovery well, and George L. Miller of the 101 Ranch. (Courtesy Conoco Inc.)

One of the first Marland Oil Company service stations was located in Marland, Oklahoma. Marland, in Noble County, three miles south of the Kay County border, was on the western edge the Three Sands Oil Field. Originally named Bliss when the post office was established in 1898, city leaders changed its name to Marland on April 8, 1922, in honor of E.W. Marland. According to Marland, the bright red Marland Oils triangle logo, seen on the pole by the driveway, came into being during World War I when he was raising money for the YMCA. When he asked permission to copyright the red triangle for industrial purposes, the YMCA granted permission out of gratitude for all that Marland had done for the organization. (Courtesy Conoco Inc.)

In the upper left of this photograph is a part of the huge tank farm that adjoined the Marland Refining Company. The tank farm held one million barrels of oil. The ability of Marland to store oil over a long period of time (until the price rose) contributed greatly to his early success. The tank cars would pull onto the siding and stop alongside the overhead spigots to be loaded from the storage tanks. (Courtesy Marland Mansion.)

The Marland Oil Company's distinctive red brick and red tile roofed service stations were highlighted by white columns at each corner. Marland Oils was one of the first companies to offer the addition of separate ladies' rest rooms at their service stations. Note the sign in the window on the right of the station, as well as at the far left corner of the building, by the curb. (Courtesy Conoco Inc.)

Constructed in 1927–1928, the Marland Mansion was built of limestone blocks and cement and cost $5,500,000. This is a view from the east side. Directly in front of the three arches was a T-shaped swimming pool. Marland and Lydie lived in the mansion for almost 18 months before he lost control of Marland Oil Company and was forced to move out of the mansion and into the artist's studio to save expenses. (Courtesy Marland's Grand Home.)

A close-up of one of the drain pipes on the Marland Mansion shows them monogramed with a capital M enclosed in a circle with the date 1927. To the right of the drain pipe is some of the ornate original wrought-iron grillwork, most of which was individually designed by John Duncan Forsyth, Marland's architect. (Author's personal collection.)

Originally the ceiling in the hallway in the gallery level of Marland's mansion was left bare, but Vincent Margliotti, a renowned Italian mural artist, volunteered to paint the ceiling. The ceiling was painted on canvas and then applied to the plaster overhead. The artist's work was so exacting that the figures are not distorted, even though the ceiling is curved. The floor is a terrazzo made of crushed marble and cement. (Courtesy Fred Marvel, Oklahoma Department of Tourism and Recreation.)

Marland's library in the east wing of the second floor has oak-paneled walls and hand-carved cornices. The windows on the east side of the room lead to a small stone balcony. On the west side of the room is a door that opens to the second story terrace and a stairway leading to the swimming pool. Around the top of the staircase, in Latin, are the words, "A man's home is his palace." (Author's personal collection.)

The poker room was located in the basement of the Marland Mansion, at the entrance to the underground passage between the mansion and the boat house and artist's studio. Marland was known for his poker playing and his evenings were often occupied with marathon poker games; however, he had a self-imposed limit on his winnings so that he would not take advantage of those who played with him. (Author's personal collection.)

The painted ceiling in the Hunt Room of the Marland Mansion depicts the history of Kay County from pre-history through 1928. The history started at the southeast corner and concluded in the northeast corner with the red triangle of the Marland Oil Company. Vincent Margliotti spent three months at the Smithsonian Institution in Washington, D.C., studying the history of the Native American inhabitants of Kay County before starting the project. (Courtesy Fred Marvel, Oklahoma Department of Tourism and Recreation.)

104

This painting of Lydie Marland hangs on the north wall of the Hunt Room. Samuel Jessurun de Mazquita, a Dutch painter who lived from 1868 until 1944, painted Lydie as Carmen, the Spanish girl in the 1874 opera by Georges Bizet. Mazquita also did a full-sized portrait of George Marland as an oilfield roustabout, dressed in torn slacks. (Courtesy Fred Marvel, Oklahoma Department of Tourism and Recreation.)

This statue of E.W. Marland, by Jo Davidson, stands on the lawn of the Ponca City Civic Center at Fifth and Grand Avenue. Davidson was brought to Ponca City by Marland to do statues of himself, Lydie and George. Davidson, who died in 1952, was best known for his likenesses of Marland, Woodrow Wilson, Franklin D. Roosevelt, Mahatma Gandhi, and Albert Einstein. (Courtesy Fred Marvel, Oklahoma Department of Tourism and Recreation.)

Unlike E.W., George Marland was an avid horseman and is shown here jumping his favorite horse, Maude. George would spend hours talking horses and their pedigrees. During the heyday of Marland Oil, polo ponies traded for high prices among Marland's friends in Ponca City. (Courtesy Marland Mansion.)

Preparing for a polo match on the field west of the Marland Mansion are, from left to right, Seward Sheldon, Curtis Allen, Dr. C.E. Northcutt, and George Marland. George enjoyed riding to the hounds on foxhunts, jumping competition and polo matches. E.W. purchased only the best polo ponies for George to ride during competition. Extra ponies were available at the Marland Mansion stables for guests who wished to participate in the matches. (Courtesy Marland Mansion.)

E.W. Marland poses on his personal horse, Tom Jones. Although Marland did not play polo, he often was seen on the grounds of the Marland Mansion riding Tom Jones along with Lydie, on her horse Rosenbar. (Courtesy Marland Mansion.)

Walter Miller, vice-president of Marland Oil Company in 1927, is shown here serving as a referee for a polo game at the Marland Mansion. Miller was known for his efficiency that made the various departments of Marland Oil operate so smoothly that by 1927 the company had a production of 13,137,048 barrels of crude annually. Like most of Marland's close associates, Miller enjoyed a passion for blooded horses. (Courtesy Marland Mansion.)

E.W. Marland was well aware of the problems of overproduction and waste in America's oil fields and played a prominent role in oil conservation and energy research. This is a photograph of the American Petroleum Institute's (API) Committee of Seven that met in the board room of Marland Oil Company in Ponca City on October 26, 1927. The API was the spokesman and primary trade organization for the oil and natural gas industry. They are, from left to right, W.S. Farish, President, Humble Oil Company; L.S. St.Claire, Union Oil Company; Marland; W.H. Ferguson, Vice-President of Continental Oil Company; William Boyd Jr., Assistant Secretary of the API; Henry McGraw, President, Gypsy Oil Company; R.E. Welsh, General Secretary of the API; James A. Veasey, Counsel of the Carter Oil Company; E.W. Clark, President of Union Oil Company and President of the API; and D.R. Richardson, General Counsel of the Marland Oil Company. (Courtesy Conoco Inc.)

To rescue his company from escalating debt, E.W. Marland sold $12 million of the company's stock to financier J.P. Morgan Jr., and granted Morgan representation on his Board of Directors. Morgan's powerful influence exerted itself on the board and Marland was forced from power. Here, Marland (center) is visibly strained as he signs documents near the end of his presidency. He resigned on November 1, 1928. (Courtesy Conoco Inc.)

Dan J. Moran was chosen by the executive committee of Marland's board as Marland's successor. Moran, thinking Marland was too lax with his employees, once slapped a man he saw sitting down, telling him to get to work. After the man slugged Moran with his fist, he informed him that he worked for the telephone company, not Marland Oil. (Courtesy Conoco Inc.)

After E.W. Marland lost control of his oil company he could no longer afford to live in the mansion. He and Lydie moved into the Artist Studio in 1930. Marland's bedroom gave him this view of his grandiose mansion. This remained their permanent home, although he and Lydie moved to the Governor's Mansion in 1934, when Marland became Oklahoma's 10th governor. (Author's personal collection.)

This is the entrance to what is now called Lydie's Cottage, but which originally was the house for Marland's chauffeur. After E.W. died in 1941, Lydie moved out of the Artist Studio and into the cottage where she lived until 1953, when she loaded her 1948 Studebaker and drove away. She returned in 1975 and again took up residency in the cottage where she lived until her death in July 1987. (Author's personal collection.)

In May of 1941, the Marland Mansion was sold to the Discalced Carmelite Fathers of Oklahoma for $66,000. Marland retained ownership of approximately three acres and a few buildings in the northwest corner of the grounds, where he lived until his death on October 3, 1941. (Courtesy Marland Mansion.)

In 1948, the Fellician Sisters of the United States of America purchased the Marland Mansion from the Discalced Carmelite Fathers for $1,500,000. Note the sisters standing on the east terrace above the swimming pool. The sisters filled in the swimming pool and all the lakes except one in the northeast corner of the mansion grounds. (Courtesy Marland Mansion.)

George Roberts Marland, shown here, joined his adopted father E.W. in the Marland Oil Company. When E.W. was forced out of the company by J.P. Morgan, George resigned in disgust. At first he maintained an office in the gate house of the estate, but eventually purchased the local Buick dealership in Ponca City which he operated for about four years, before moving to Tulsa where he became an independent oil broker. (Courtesy Marland Mansion.)

Kansas Governor Alf Landon (left) visits with Lydie Marland and Oklahoma's governor, E.W. Marland. Landon served as governor in Kansas from 1933–1937, while Marland was elected to the U.S. House of Representatives in 1932, and elected as governor in 1934. In 1936, Landon ran for President, while Marland made his bid for the U.S. Senate. Both were unsuccessful. (Courtesy Conoco Inc.)

Seven

PONCA CITY

The post office at New Ponca was opened on January 12, 1894, with the "New" added to distinguish it from the post office at the Ponca Indian Agency, five miles to the south. In 1896, the Indian Agency post office changed its name to White Eagle and two years later, on July 7, 1898, New Ponca was renamed Ponca. On October 12, 1913, "City" was added.

A mile north of Ponca City was the community of Cross, which rivaled Ponca City. Cross was created on the day of the opening of the Cherokee Outlet and by the afternoon of September 16, 1893, had a population of 1,500. The railroad station at Cross was located in an unused railroad boxcar and residents of Ponca City had to travel to Cross to board the train. Supposedly, one night in September of 1894, a mob from Ponca City invaded Cross and pulled the boxcar depot a mile to Ponca City. Eventually, most of the major businesses in Cross followed this move to Ponca City.

The stories of shallow deposits of natural gas were well known in the area around Ponca City. These stories reached E.W. Marland, who arrived in December of 1908 to examine the region for signs of underground wealth. In the spring of 1910, Marland opened the area around Ponca City to major gas production and seven years later oil development started. Marland was on his way to becoming a petroleum legend, and Ponca City soon developed into a major energy center.

A crowd of onlookers waits for the first Atchison, Topeka, and Santa Fe Railroad train at the new depot in Ponca City at 9:27 a.m., September 22, 1894. The depot had been located in a boxcar at Cross, a mile north of Ponca City. When railway officials refused to open another depot in Ponca City, local leaders physically moved the boxcar from Cross to Ponca City one night in September of 1894. (Courtesy Top of Oklahoma Museum.)

This is the interior of a Ponca City saloon in 1898, prior to the passage of prohibition, when Oklahoma became a state in 1907. Although the saloons were closed on November 16, 1907, and the liquor and beer either shipped out of state or dumped, Ponca City still retained much of its Wild West atmosphere when E.W. Marland stepped off the train in 1908. (Courtesy Marland's Grand Home.)

This Harness & Saddles shop and Dry Goods and Grocery store in Ponca City's business district, c. 1900, were typical of the wood frame, false-fronted buildings that initially formed the community's business district. The Dry Good and Grocery store also advertised a restaurant offering lemonade and ice cream. (Courtesy Pioneer Woman Museum.)

Located in the middle of Grand Avenue, just to the end of First Street, was Ponca City's first municipal water well, powered by a windmill, and tank. Prior to the drilling of the well, Ponca Citians were dependent on a spring, three-quarters of a mile from town on William "Water Billy" Evans' land. He delivered water to homes and businesses for 15¢ a barrel. (Courtesy Pioneer Woman Museum.)

This was Ponca City's First National Bank, c. 1900–1905. By this time Ponca City's original dirt streets had been paved with bricks, provided by Charles Welch's brick yard. Note the electric power pole in front of the bank. By July 1894, barely ten months after the land run opening the region to settlement, Ponca City became the first community in the old Cherokee Outlet to have electric lights. (Courtesy Pioneer Woman Museum.)

Early in the community's history, local boosters announced their intention to transform the town from a frontier settlement into a bustling, booming city. The discovery of oil nearby pumped millions of dollars into the community's economy and resulted in the establishment of a multitude of civic improvements, such as the Ponca City Band, seen here c. 1907–1910. (Courtesy Marland's Grand Home.)

These workers are completing the construction of the cut stone bridge at Fourteenth Street and Highland Avenue. Kay County was the center of a major stone quarrying industry during the territorial period and supplied most of the cut stone used in Oklahoma Territory. Much of the cut stone used locally came from Rush Elmore's quarry. J.C. Armstrong, Miles Fuller, Jesse C. Feagin, and John Berry also operated quarries in the area. (Courtesy Pioneer Woman Museum.)

The Koller Hardware Company occupied both floors of its building in downtown Ponca City, while next door two doctors and a dentist maintained offices above the McDowell and Castator Drug Store. Seen here, the driver of the Ponca City Ice Company wagon is taking out blocks of ice for delivery. Note the cover worn by the horse advertising the Ponca City Drug Company. The ice company was owned by J.L. McCarthy. (Courtesy Pioneer Woman Museum.)

Located at the intersection of First Street and Grand Avenue in Ponca City, the Arcade Hotel offered the city's finest accommodations for decades. Originally located in Cross, the hotel, initially a square wooden building, was moved to Ponca in 1894. E.W. and Mary Virginia Marland lived in a three-room suite on the ground floor. Jackie McFarland Laird was the chef and her 65¢ T-bone steak became famous. The Arcade Hotel was demolished in 1974. (Courtesy Pioneer Woman Museum.)

Row houses, such as these in south Ponca City during the heyday of the Kay County oil boom, were much more substantial than the shotgun houses typical of the early boom years. Many oil companies built such houses to attract permanent employees who wanted to bring their families with them. It was common for the row houses to be painted the "company color." Note the identical design of the houses. (Courtesy Allen Muchmore.)

Blanche Lucas was the wife of Frank Lucas, one of E.W. Marland's confidants and an official of the Marland Oil Company. Lucas was also the Ponca City postmaster. When he died, Blanche replaced him as postmaster. She was also one of the principle organizers of the Women's Clubs of Oklahoma. Their home on Hillcrest was built at the same time as Marland's mansion and used the same stone. (Courtesy Pioneer Woman Museum.)

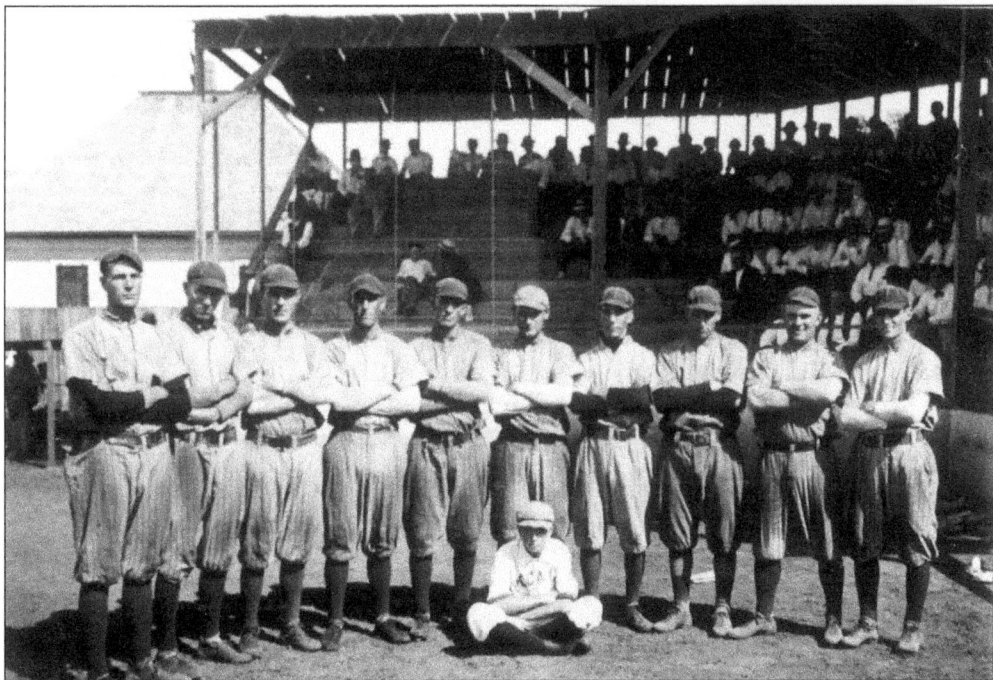

Ponca City fielded its first town baseball team in 1894. This is a team photograph of the 1914 O-K League championship team from Ponca City. After winning the championship, the team barnstormed through northern Oklahoma and southern Kansas playing other local teams on Sunday afternoon. (Courtesy Pioneer Woman Museum.)

The Ponca City tornado of April 25, 1912, was photographed by Jerry Drake. The funnel formed west of Ponca City near Bill Vanselous' Big V Ranch about 4:45 in the afternoon. After it was initially sighted, it took almost 15 minutes for the tornado to travel to Ponca City. When Drake heard about the funnel he hurriedly set up his camera and captured this photograph as it approached. (Courtesy Pioneer Woman Museum.)

This photograph shows the path of destruction left by the April 25, 1912 tornado that roared into Ponca City from the southwest at about 5:00 in the afternoon. With almost 15 minutes of warning most people found shelter; however, one woman was killed by falling debris. The funnel passed through the Wylde Addition, to the west of the Atchison, Topeka & Santa Fe Railroad, across the northern portion of Ponca City. (Courtesy Pioneer Woman Museum.)

MUNICIPAL BUILDING, AT PONCA CITY, OKLAHOMA.

The Ponca City Civic Center and Municipal Building was originally built on Grand Avenue in 1917, and included a city hall and civic center best known for its bell tower and fire tower. Four years later, two wings were added to house the local police and fire stations. Mae West, Duke Ellington, Jack Benny, John Phillip Sousa, and Will Rogers were among some of the entertainers who played the Civic Center. (Courtesy Oklahoma Heritage Association.)

The original Ponca City hospital was founded by the local Chamber of Commerce in 1919. In 1921, the sisters of St. Joseph in Wichita, Kansas assumed management of the facility. This building, usually referred to as the "hospital on the hill," was built in 1925 at a cost of $250,000, most of which was underwritten by E.W. Marland. The hospital was called "ideal" by the National Assemblage of Surgeons when it opened. (Courtesy Marland Mansion.)

This is a photograph of Lew Wentz at the peak of his career. Unlike E.W. Marland, Wentz was shrewd and thrifty. He was a generous individual who shunned the limelight. His annual distribution of toys to the poorer children of Ponca City became a citywide event. He also provided shoes to needy children and outwitted the local school superintendent, who vainly attempted to discover the identity of the anonymous donor. (Courtesy Marland's Grand Home.)

These Ponca City firemen are preparing to deliver Christmas trees donated by Lew Wentz during the 1929 holiday season. Before he became wealthy, Wentz would borrow money to provide Christmas presents for the less fortunate children of Ponca City. During the Great Depression, Wentz allowed free admission to his movie theater to children whose parents could not afford the cost of admission. (Courtesy Pioneer Woman Museum.)

This is a view of Lew Wentz Recreational Camp's swimming pool in 1938. Twin towers flank the entrance to the stone and marble steps and benches leading to the pool, which was elevated and surrounded by an ornate wall. The dressing rooms were located below ground. The pool measured 100-by-50 feet and had electric lights at the bottom. The towers were 80 feet tall and were accessible by ladder. (Courtesy Pioneer Woman Museum.)

This is an overview of the Marland Oil Refinery in the 1920s. When the refinery opened in 1918 the company owned and operated 320 railroad tank cars. By 1926, the company owned 998 tank cars and leased another 3,200 cars and contained storage tanks capable of holding ten million barrels of oil. (Courtesy Conoco Inc.)

This is an aerial view of the Ponca Military Academy, which was originally founded by E.W. Marland as the Marland Industrial Institute as an in-house school and country club. In 1940, Colonel and Mrs. William V. Cox purchased the property and transformed it into the Ponca Military Academy. During World War II, British pilots of the Royal Air Force were housed there while training at the Ponca City Municipal Airport. (Courtesy Pioneer Woman Museum.)

Work on the Marland Mansion started in 1925, and when it was finished in June of 1928 E.W. threw the doors open to all who wished to see his new home. This is a portion of the crowd that made its way through the mansion during its open house. The two windows in the upper left are in Marland's sitting room, which had doors opening onto the upper terrace where a crowd is standing. (Author's personal collection.)

The Poncan Theatre, seen here, was built in 1927 as the fifth and grandest theatre in Ponca City. Four men—George Brett, Eugene Wetzel, Dr. J.A. Douglass and C.F. Calkins—formed a company to build it. It was designed for theatre and film, featuring a $22,000 Wurlitzer organ. The theatre was designed in a Spanish Colonial Revival style with the interior mimicking an outdoor Mediterranean courtyard. (Courtesy Fred Marvel, Oklahoma Department of Tourism and Recreation.)

The Marland family lived in what was known as Marland's Grand Home for 12 years. The home continued to be a private residence until 1967, when it was purchased by the City. It now houses the Daughters of the American Revolution Memorial Museum; memorabilia from the world-famous Miller brothers' 101 Ranch; and collections from area tribes. The ground level remains reminiscent of the days it was occupied by Marland. (Courtesy Fred Marvel, Oklahoma Department of Tourism and Recreation.)

With the depressed oil prices of the 1930s came an increased demand to end the wasteful practices of overproduction. In an effort to bring stability to the industry, Oklahoma Governor E.W. Marland convened a series of conferences of representatives of oil-producing states at his mansion in Ponca City. The final meeting was held on January 3, 1935, and from it stemmed the Interstate Oil Compact Commission. The delegates to this final meeting are pictured here, from left to right, as follows: (front row) Jack Blalock, Tom C. Johnson, William Bell, Ernest W. Marland, E.B. Shawver, unidentified, Hiram Dow, and John E. Farrelwere; (back row) Northcutt Ely, Herbert Kent, Charley C. Brown, J.W. Olvey, Jeff Davis, Wirt Franklin, Mac A. Williamson, George Marland, W.J. Holloway, Patrick J. Hurley, Ralph Cummins, C.V. Terrell, and unidentified. (Courtesy Interstate Oil Compact Commission.)

Searching for a way to transport natural gas from areas where a pipeline was not feasible led to the discovery of a process of turning the gas into liquid. Here, Randy Adkins, a technician in the gas-to-liquid lab at Conoco Inc., pours some of the liquid into a vial for more testing. (Courtesy Conoco Inc.)

Felicia Gertken works in the carbon fiber lab at Conoco Inc. in Ponca City. In this photograph she is holding the carbon fiber which, although extremely lightweight, is as strong or stronger than steel. The carbon fiber is being tested for a number of uses, including construction of buildings and roadways. The new carbon fiber plant in Ponca City may well pave the way into the future. (Courtesy Conoco Inc.)